Sharing Christ With Others

When You're Not Good at It

Sharing Christ With Others

When You're Not Good at It

by

Gene Edwards

Copyright © 2024 Cindy Edwards

All rights reserved. No part of this book may be reproduced or used in any manner without the prior written permission of the copyright owner, except for the use of brief quotations. These are the author's memories, from his perspective, and the events have been represented as faithfully as possible.

ISBN: 978-1-950891-23-8

www.seedsowers.com

Dedication

To Scott Kurkian
Who was a constant encouragement
to get this book published,
&
Who is an enduring friend to
SeedSowers Publishing House

TABLE OF CONTENTS

Dedication --- v

Foreword --- ix

Chapter 1: Memories of Failures ------------------ 1

Chapter 2: What Happened Next -------------- 11

Chapter 3: The Key ------------------------------ 19

Chapter 4: The Transition ---------------------- 27

Chapter 5: The Name --------------------------- 39

Chapter 6: Singing Your Way Into Jesus ------ 43

Chapter 7: The Unbelievable -------------------- 53

Foreword

Gene Edwards penned this book not long before his death in 2022. His heart was to alleviate the fear of sharing Christ, for even shy people. He said there is no reason for it to seem so difficult to guide a friend or stranger all the way through to the moments of actually receiving Jesus into their heart. Gene spent the early years of his ministry winning people to Christ and teaching others, including ministers, how to share the good news of Christ with others. In this book you will read about his ministry, and you will learn some easy ways to share your faith with others.

Foreword

In Gene's later ministry, he sought to help Christians and indigenous churches provide a healthy environment for new believers to grow in their faith. He wrote books and spoke in conferences about restoring church practice to the way it was experienced in the first century, when so many new believers were gathering together in ekklesia.

In this book, Gene presents a very simple approach to soulwinning, enabling simple, perhaps even introverted Christians, to be able to share their faith and actually lead someone to receive Christ as Lord of their life.

We pray you will put these tools into practice and share Christ with those whose lives you touch.

From the publisher
SeedSowers

CHAPTER 1

MEMORIES OF FAILURES

Let's begin with a confession. About 95% of the Christians in this world are shy about witnessing to someone else, especially when the person is a stranger.

We are all a little bit reluctant to offend someone, and most Christians are even reluctant to talk about Jesus Christ. Still, you are sure you are supposed to be leading people to a saving knowledge of Jesus Christ.

I happen to fall in the class of being a Christian extrovert. Extroverts have the reputation of being able to walk up to perfect

Chapter 1- Memories Of Failures

strangers, start a conversation about anything, and do so without any hesitation. But have you not heard? Inside every extrovert is an introvert. I am just such a person. Speaking for virtually all extroverts—though there are some true extroverts out there who are exceptions to the rule—most of us extroverts find it very difficult to begin a conversation with a perfect stranger about something as personal as our relationship to the Lord.

This whole book was written very deliberately for the genuinely shy. To turn a person who is genuinely shy into a soul winner to Jesus Christ is not easy. You are going to have to work at it. You are going to have to be deliberate in your quest to lead others to Christ. Nonetheless, this is not an impossible task.

I am presenting myself to you as exhibit "A." Today I am a very old man. I have been speaking to others about Christ most of my Christian life. Nonetheless, there were agonies in getting started. I deliberately set out to find out why I was a colossal failure at being a witness to my wonderful Lord. Guilt was deep and I was not really certain that I would be able to talk to others about Christ in a way that was friendly, warm and natural.

Let's go back to my youth. I was a college and seminary graduate. I took all the courses in evangelism that my seminary offered. Yet, nothing I had been taught broke my reluctance to witness. Whatever I tried simply did not work.

If you ever should be in east Texas and find yourself between Sulphur Springs and Winnsboro, you will come across a little town called Pickton. My car was parked in the front yard of the church in Pickton. I was trying to witness to a young man who was straddling the fender of an antique car. When he realized I was about to start talking about "getting saved," he jumped off that fender, landed facing me, saying, "No, no, no, I'm not interested!"

Chapter 1- Memories Of Failures

That was a turning point in my life. I made a decision, and what a decision it turned out to be. I started making inquiries: "Who are the most effective personal soul winners in the United States?" I accumulated a list of the names of such men, their addresses and telephone numbers. I decided that I was going to get in a car or train or airplane and meet as many of those men as I could. Further, I would be asking them to go door to door with me. I wanted to watch how they so effectively led others to Jesus Christ.

The most meaningful encounter, which overshadowed all others, was the day I met Hubert Mitchell in a place called The Loop in downtown Chicago. Hubert Mitchell was in a class by himself. He treated The Loop as though it were a country church in a country village. It is in fact a giant group of skyscrapers. He walked down the streets of The Loop like he owned the place. The Loop was Hubert's parish. He and I walked into a skyscraper. He walked over to the elevators and punched the topmost button. We were going to the penthouse. Quite frankly, I thought that Hubert had lost his mind.

The elevator doors opened, not to a room nor to an office, but to the entire top floor of the building! The receptionist greeted us warmly.

I had absolutely no idea what Hubert was about to do. Hubert was a deep throated, very self-assured human being. Certainly, I had picked the wrong man to find out how a shy person shares about their Lord.

He announced, "My name is Hubert Mitchell. I would like to talk with the president of this company. I'd like to have a word of prayer with him."

There I was in my early twenties, born and raised in east Texas. I was absolutely certain we were about to be thrown out. The receptionist was astounded. She pressed a button.

"Mr. [President]," referring to the man who owned the building, "Mr. [President], sir, there is a man out here who is asking to come into your office to have a word of prayer."

I recall that I heard the clear voice of the man who owned that building, saying three words, "Send him in."

The receptionist escorted Hubert to what was obviously the largest office in the building.

What did I do? Absolutely nothing. I had just turned into a pillar of salt.

About forty-five minutes later, Hubert came back. I knew what he was like. He not only treated downtown Loop as his parish, he also spent time virtually every day going from floor to floor asking to pray for whoever was the person in charge of that floor. He led a great number of people to the Lord, and on Wednesday at noon all his converts met together for lunch.

I never asked a single question. Whether or not that man had actually been led to Christ, I still do not know even unto today. Hubert simply announced, "He will be with us Wednesday for lunch."

That evening I had dinner with Hubert's family. They were all former missionaries. Then we started going door-to-door in a neighborhood where he himself had never been.

We knocked on doors, and he would say exactly the same thing. "My name is Hubert Mitchell and this young man is named Gene. We would like to ask if we could come in and have a word of prayer with you."

Well, we Texans are very friendly people, but I was expecting to be thrown into the street in cold Chicago.

We were invited in. I watched Hubert Mitchell lead a man and his wife to the Lord Jesus Christ.

I knew that Hubert taught soulwinning to others. I heard the way he led people to Christ. It was not in the traditional way of quoting verses, getting somebody to bow their head and ask Christ to come into their heart, both the witness and the sinner with their eyes closed, both repeating the "sinner's prayer." All of these things were familiar to me.

No, I watched Hubert Mitchell throw the book away. I learned that night that everything Hubert did was contrary to everything I had ever been taught or read about. He did not get a Bible out. He did not quote Scripture. Now that was certainly contrary to everything I had learned in every class and in every book on evangelism to which I had ever been exposed.

I learned something so valuable that day that it was, in fact, life changing. It was not the power of Scripture that would draw someone to Christ. Quoting Scripture to someone who is not familiar with Jesus Christ will find you in an argument with almost certainty. Hubert talked about Jesus Christ. This man was speaking to a young couple about someone he felt personally familiar with. That was his Lord and Savior Jesus Christ. Nothing less than the Lord Jesus Christ. There was not one thing that Hubert did right that night. It was contrary to everything I learned about being an effective witness.

During my search for soul winners, I met some of the most effective people who existed on this earth, but it was this night that changed my understanding of leading someone to Christ.

Only one of those men would you call a total extrovert. His name was Jack. When Jack stopped to get gasoline, when he would meet anybody at anytime, anywhere, he would ask one question right out of the blue: "If you died right now, would you go to heaven or hell?"

Now, I have watched Jack lead others to Jesus Christ, but I have never once asked that question of anyone!

Jack's words were effective, but Jack was a true extrovert, comfortable in any situation in which he might find himself.

Chapter 1- Memories Of Failures

What can you do as a shy Christian to be able to meet a perfect stranger and end up actually bringing him to the Lord Jesus Christ? If you, a shy person, are going to be able to pick up this beautiful role of leading others to know your savior, you are going to have to spend some time teaching yourself and probably asking another Christian to play the role of someone who is not a believer, so you can practice. Yes, it will take that much effort.

There is one thing you can do. Get some paper, sit down and write out the words you feel you could use to move from an ordinary conversation to a conversation that might have eternal consequences.

Give time to this. Approach it from several views. Recall your own salvation experience. What does Jesus Christ mean to your life on this very day.

CHAPTER 2

What Happened Next

Having completed my venture to find effective soul winners, I went back to east Texas to the Tabernacle Baptist Church. I began leading people to Jesus Christ. Some of those people came to the Sunday morning meetings. They definitely did not fit in. There is a bit of an adjustment to see prostitutes and drunks filling the pews in the Sunday morning church service.

Soon pastors began inviting me to speak to their congregations. Beautiful results followed.

I was invited to speak in large and influential churches on weekends about leading others to Jesus Christ. I even wrote a book about how to win souls. The book, unlikely as it might seem, became a best seller by the standards of that day.

I received a phone call from the head of the Department of Evangelism of the Assemblies of God located in Missouri. He made a very simple proposition, "Gene, would you be willing to hold a citywide campaign in Wisconsin in March? There will be about twenty-five to thirty Assemblies of God churches joining together. We will see if this works."

I accepted. March in Wisconsin is "North Pole-ish." I have never in my life seen anything that cold. Sure enough, I spent one week teaching Christians from over twenty assemblies how to lead people to Jesus Christ. I threw the traditional book away, and it would be impossible to explain what came as a result. A large number of charismatics went door-to-door in the largest city in Wisconsin on Friday night after a week of

Chapter 2- What Happened Next

training. Everybody returned on Saturday night to share their experience. These meetings were some of the hottest pentecostal meetings you will ever see. No, it was not tongues, nor enthusiastic worship. These were people who were jubilant about leading someone to Jesus Christ.

Who were the most excited people in the room? Pastors, pastors, and more pastors. Men were leading people to Jesus Christ who, though they were ministers, had never led anyone to Christ in their entire lives.

Word reached Assemblies of God churches throughout the United States. I was suddenly nationally famous.

This went on for about a year. Even my own denomination, Baptists, heard and became jealous and invited me, an unknown minister from Hopkins County, to speak at a large conference. So it was to a large city, the Baptists invited an almost unknown man to direct a citywide campaign in door-to-door evangelism.

Chapter 2- What Happened Next

They would meet on Saturday night for everyone to share what they had experienced going door-to-door. The stories were breathtaking. Some stories were unbelievable.

I shall never forget what happened in one case. Between Sunday school and the gathering of the congregation, one of the businessmen decided to go back and check on his office. Sure enough, there was a burglar present. The businessman reached for his gun. The would-be thief was a terrified teenager. The businessman invited the teenager, at gunpoint, to sit down and hear about Jesus Christ. The young burglar received Christ as his savior. I know he was soundly converted because I met that young man. He became a member of the church where that gun-toting Christian was a member. This teenager had indeed come to the Lord Jesus Christ and was as devout a convert to Christ as anyone could ever expect to be.

Chapter 2- What Happened Next

The meetings where Christians told their experiences of leading people to Christ in living rooms were a "hoe-down," that is, some of the most wonderful meetings anyone had ever attended. I began receiving citywide campaign invitations as far away as California to the west and New England to the east.

In New England, the situation was very unusual, as there were no large groups of Baptists or charismatics. These were individual churches that in their struggle to survive had created ministerial alliances of all the evangelical churches.

I thought surely I had come to the peak when I began being invited to campaigns in New England. There was one place that nobody ever got invited to. Though there was no citywide campaign there, I was invited to Washington, D.C. to meet with individual devout Christian senators and congressmen.

Chapter 2- What Happened Next

Until this day, I have never made any reference public or private about the time I spent in Washington. I will tell you one thing. I ended up in a very large photo, not on the cover, but on the inside of Time Magazine, talking to a president of the United States about his relationship to Jesus Christ.

For virtually five years, I was hardly ever home. I spoke in so many seminaries, Bible schools, and conventions, I lost count. I came to hold a rather unusual position: that is, I have trained more Christians to witness for Jesus Christ than anyone ever had. These were citywide campaigns in personal evangelism, the like of which had never been known before or since.

That changed when I was struck down with a disease called disseminated histoplasmosis. There were no reliable statistics on how many people died of that disease, but I was told that the chance of recovery was less than one percent. It is a deadly fungus that moves throughout the body as does cancer. There was no known cure nor treatment at that time. That brought an end to that ministry. I was in one degree or another of convalescence for at least seven years. I did not speak publicly for five years. When I did, it was almost as though it was two different individuals. I even looked physically different. I cannot even say, here as I am approaching ninety years of age, that I am fully recovered, nor will I ever be. As Jacob had a broken hip, so also this Jacob very definitely has "had a broken hip."

Now, it is time that you and I begin talking about how to deal with your shyness. There are things you can do that can break your shyness.

There are simple ways by which even the most shy person can witness to the love of God in Christ Jesus.

CHAPTER 3

The Key

There may be pastors or ministers wondering exactly where to begin. We all start at exactly the same place. That place is coming out of your shell.

For example, we know little of the existence of our waiter or waitress, while we spend close to an hour or longer with them every time we eat at a restaurant. I try to know the name of my server. If I hear their name and it sounds in any way foreign or unusual, I will inquire as to the unusual nature of the name or the accent.

Chapter 3- The Key

Whenever I meet someone who has a Bible name, or even if I think it is a Bible name, I ask them, "Was that a deliberate choice on the part of your parents?" I would say that if you have met someone with a Bible name, the chances are that about half of those people will either be from a very religious home or their parents are out-and-out Christians. The other half have no idea their name is a Bible name and were probably named after some distant relative. But always, I discover one thing, the fact that I am paying attention to that person enlightens their life. When I return to that restaurant, I try to remember which server I met with and what their name was. In the beginning, this was not natural to me. It is now. Many people do not want to know other people. They want to eat their food and leave. What opportunities we have lost, to come to know people. The very fact that I am friendly makes them friendly toward me.

I do not feel that it is my business to steal from a server's wages; therefore, I do not witness

Chapter 3- The Key

to folks who wait on me at meal times. If there are exceptions to that, those exceptions will make themselves known; but I will not jeopardize someone's job by taking the moments away that would be necessary to actually lead them through the salvation experience. Nonetheless, there are such opportunities that present themselves in an unusual way. This includes the person who sells me my groceries.

One of the first things you have to do is to deliberately come out of your shell. Point one: start talking to people who are physically near you.

If I see someone in an unusual situation, such as sitting down on the sidewalk with what looks like no visible means of support, there is a good chance I will sit down beside them and start a conversation with them.

In other words, from the time I get up in the morning until I go to bed, I want to make sure that I have not passed up an opportunity to

Chapter 3- The Key

at least meet someone. I try to make sure I am not doing this just to be friendly. I have purpose, and that is to see an opening to talk to someone about Jesus Christ. Such openings come in a thousand different ways. Most of them are because you create the opening, and others because they simply present themselves.

I received an anonymous call from someone on a jury. I knew exactly who the caller was by their voice. They made no identification, and said, "There is someone in jail who really wants and needs the Lord and has asked somebody to help him." A few minutes later, the telephone rang, and I heard another familiar voice concerning the same young man. I went to the jail and told them I would like to talk for a moment to the gentleman who was on trial. I was allowed to visit with the young man for a few minutes. It was exactly as had been described to me. He wanted Jesus Christ to come into his heart, and he made it pretty obvious to the jury. I explained the "how

Chapter 3- The Key

to" of receiving Christ. You might call him the man who witnessed himself right into salvation.

While we are discussing exceptional people and exceptional circumstances, I might be in a situation where I am strongly rebuffed and clearly rejected. In such an unusual instance, I make no effort to go any further. The heart is set, period.

There are thousands of people around us in our lifetime who, whether we realize it or not, simply need to be shown the "how to" to receive Jesus Christ.

It is going to be your responsibility after reading this book, to learn to tell others how to know Jesus Christ. We will discuss that a little later, but it is for you to practice and learn, either in front of a mirror or on the side of your bed, and learn how to walk someone through receiving Christ.

Those campaigns in door-to-door evangelism were very effective. Why? There was one thing which was certain: Everyone had to

Chapter 3- The Key

practice. Everyone in the training paired off in twos. Christian Number One would practice leading Christian Number Two to the Lord. After that, they would reverse roles: Christian Number Two would lead Christian Number One to the Lord.

Because these campaigns were usually a week long, by the time we came to Friday, everyone was practiced in leading one other person through the conversion experience.

You are shy. On this one occasion, you must practice. Find a Christian friend and "lead that person to Christ!" Reverse roles several times. If you do not practice, the chances are that you will never lead anyone through the experience of accepting Jesus Christ.

No, this is not easy; yet you will find practicing to be extremely helpful. Chisel that in stone. If you practice, you may find yourself no less than a soul winner. The key, as I have noted for over half a century, is very practical: Practice!

Chapter 3- The Key

Now, for the moment when you will face the problem of how to get started.

CHAPTER 4

The Transition

We are faced with the simple problem of how to get started.

You are having a conversation, simple and comfortable. Now you want to transition into talking about the Lord Jesus Christ, and then even go a step further beyond that, to actually lead them through receiving Jesus Christ. No wonder so many Christians are shy about witnessing. This is a pretty tall order.

Let's take this a little bit slow. I have spent over fifty years thinking about this subject and considering how to help other Christians make

Chapter 4- The Transition

that transition. This is where you are going to have to do some practicing.

I am going to introduce to you a planned way of doing this transition. It is familiar to me and probably hundreds of thousands of other Christians. It was written by a brother named Bill, a cherished friend of mine a long time ago. What he wrote was a breakthrough for many Christians. There is an excellent chance you may have heard about it.

The conversation turns to a transitional statement, "Have you ever heard of the four spiritual laws?" There have been hundreds of thousands of people led to Jesus Christ by that simple transitional statement.

How do you get a copy of the four spiritual laws? The task is very simple. If you know how to use a computer (everyone does except me), you can simply go to your computer and type in four spiritual laws. A few moments later, you will have in print that work which has been so much help

Chapter 4- The Transition

to so many people. It is my understanding that the small pamphlet is available.

I ask you to please read the pamphlet. Read it slowly, read it again. You may want to practice this transitional phrasing that is so easily usable, "Have you ever heard of the four spiritual laws?" Take a very good look at what Bill has done here. Unlike other evangelistic tools used through the centuries, Bill has not belabored our sinful state.

I want to address that for a moment. I published a book entitled *The Story of My Life as Told by Jesus Christ*. This is a book which blends the four Gospels.

In the Gospels, it is surprising how many times the Lord does not make reference to sin. In fact, in the four Gospels, when they are blended together into one complete whole, you discover that Jesus Christ's major topic of conversation is the Lord Jesus Christ! This is what I have learned from so many masters of soul winning and also from the greatest One of all.

Chapter 4- The Transition

Become familiar with the four spiritual laws. Stop and consider, what might you be able to say to a perfect stranger.

Let's say that you are shy. Let us say that the great overwhelming majority of us find it difficult to change the subject enough that it will eventually lead to our telling someone about Jesus Christ and to his or her receiving Him as savior.

No cheating: this book was not written about people talking to others about Christ. The purpose of this book is to actually carry someone through the experience of receiving Jesus Christ as Lord and Savior. That is a high hill to climb for very shy people.

Give it some thought. What do you think? With a great deal of forethought, some practice, and perhaps even writing down your words, you might come up with something that you feel would be comfortable for you to say to someone about the Lord.

Chapter 4- The Transition

This has become a frequent thought of mine. What are some ways I might transition a conversation to the subject of finding out if the person is a Christian or has given some thought to being a Christian, or knows little about the meaning of salvation in Christ. Of course, there is always the rare person who is belligerent and wants you to know they are at least an atheist, and maybe belligerently vocal about it.

If a person is willing to listen, may I suggest another way of making transition. You could begin by saying, "There are three principles by which I live. May I share them with you?" You have your experience with your Lord. Personally, my salvation took place in a cemetery, all alone.

I will not hesitate to say, "Today I am ninety years old and I have learned three things about life. May I share them with you?"

This very day, as I was writing this page in this book, I decided that I would give some thought to this: that if I were to have an

Chapter 4- The Transition

opportunity today to witness, exactly what would I do and do it naturally? This is what I am about to write to you.

Please understand that this is how I might talk to someone today about Jesus Christ. I would say the following:

"Life on this planet is too tough to survive. I do not have the capacity to deal with some of the crises which arrive in my life and will come to me between now and the time I die. I think this is the fact that everyone, all of us, will have discovered by the time we are fifty or sixty, about the experience of living on this earth. The problems are bigger than I am. So much unhappiness, so much divorce, so much betrayal. I need someone bigger than I am. I met that person, a long time ago. He did not give me a crutch to lean on to get through the dark hours or the trials or tribulations. This is something many people do not understand. This person gave me a life higher than the human species, and placed that higher

Chapter 4- The Transition

life in me. Every day I draw from the life higher than human life. He offers you that same life. I am not speaking of leading a good life or becoming a Christian, which is usually considered a day when someone says, 'from this day forward, I am not going to cuss, smoke or chew.' That is not the life that is inside of me. If I cuss, lie, cheat, smoke and was addicted to alcohol or taking drugs, changing that is not what becoming a Christian means. What it means is that somebody a lot bigger than I am, more powerful, comes into my life, and all on His own, He changes me from being one thing into another. So instead of a long list of things you do or do not do, He gives you a gift. That gift is His own divine life that will live inside of you. He does the changing without any conditions. He gives you His own divine life. This has nothing to do with getting dressed up and going to church on Sunday morning. It does not have anything to do with bad or good. It has to do with divine life over human life."

I have no idea what the rest of this day holds. This I can tell you, I will be almost completely comfortable if there is a situation that allows me to speak about Jesus Christ, my Lord.

Why did I phrase it with the words almost completely comfortable? I do not want to be totally comfortable in sharing Christ with someone. I want to be keenly aware that I am talking to a real human being who has life struggles, whether he be an angry atheist or someone who has no education whatsoever, I want to be able to keep in mind that this is a living, breathing soul who has a history to his life. I will never be so comfortable that I am more interested in witnessing than I am of introducing my Lord Jesus to enter and dwell in the life of that person for the rest of their life.

Let me share this with you: once you begin talking to others about your Lord and Savior, you will become more comfortable. About how many times does it take? I would say a minimum of ten times. Somewhere in those ten people, you are almost certain to ask someone to actually receive Christ inside their inmost being. Then you will know that it is possible for even you to talk to someone about the Lord without having a heart attack or a fainting spell.

This matter of transitioning from one subject to another is so critically important to your witness here on earth, that you, and you alone, are going to have to deal with this matter until you find something that you might be semi-comfortable in saying to someone.

Personally, I am most comfortable simply by saying, "There is something I would like to tell you if you do not mind. It was the most important moment I ever lived, and it changed everything about me. May I tell you what it is?"

The number of people who are willing to listen to you is awesome. I have met people who have never heard of God. I have met people who only vaguely know that there is a God, and I have received responses such as this: "Oh, you want

Chapter 4- The Transition

to talk to me about the Lord Jesus Christ? That is wonderful, because I also know Him. Tell me how it happened in your life, and I will tell you how it happened in mine!"

Work on that transition. Come back six months later and try again and see where you are. Let a year pass and sit down and ask yourself, "Where am I now, today at this moment, in the matter of learning how to move a casual conversation to talking to someone about my Lord and Savior, Jesus Christ." Though progress might be small, you know that you have started. You are on your way to breaking through being able to speak to someone about what Jesus Christ means to you.

This book was written for you. We have come down to one simple matter, and that matter is whether or not you will give attention in your own life, as a shy Christian, to make the effort to being able to move the conversation onto the subject of your Lord. I have said, write it down, speak it out loud, practice what you have written on a fellow Christian. Remember, you may have to try several times to turn a conversation to Christ before you are comfortable enough to speak to a stranger about the Lord.

CHAPTER 5

The Name

I would like to share with you one way, the simplest way, of receiving Jesus Christ. This I attribute to nothing more than the power of a divine word. That word, one and only one word, is *Jesus*. I have shared this word with governors, congressmen and senators. I have shared it with young people, adults and elderly people. The word is Jesus. I realize that there are some fairly strict conditions in which I would do this; nonetheless, it does seem to happen quite frequently.

When I know that someone, as best I can discern, is going to open their heart to the Lord Jesus Christ, I say to that person, "I want you to say just one word. That word is Jesus." I will not go any further than this except to say, I say again, "Speak that word. Speak it again. Say it again." This time if that person does speak His name, I ask him to add the word Lord. I hear a change in their voice. "Say Lord Jesus. Say it again. Say 'Dear Lord Jesus.' Now say it again. This time say, 'Dear Lord Jesus, I love you.' Say it again. This time say, 'Lord Jesus, I love you. I love you.'"

Never forget what you just read. The repeating of the word Jesus is powerful. It is a rare person who can withstand the power of that name. I doubt that you question that.

I would encourage you, dear Christian, to get in a room and close the door with no one else around. Just start saying quietly and gently, Jesus, and then add to it Lord Jesus. Add to that Dear Lord Jesus. Say it lovingly, tenderly. Drive everything else out of your mind and just love Him.

Chapter 5- The Name

How many times we have even written songs about all You want me to do, Lord, is to serve You. I really question that to be scripturally correct, although I have been called of God to serve the Lord Jesus Christ. The first and greatest commandment is to love your Lord. So, while you are sitting there alone, just tell your Lord: "I love you, Lord Jesus. I love you, Lord. I love you, Jesus. My Lord and my God, I love you." Alone in my room, while driving my car, or walking down the sidewalk, I still whisper one word, Jesus. I speak His name passionately, and that name alone tends to consume me. I have known that name for seventy years.

I am ninety years old and I still cry when I tell the Lord that I love Him.

I think you will find it very easy and very comfortable to transition from saying the word Jesus to asking someone else to say His name with you.

CHAPTER 6

SINGING YOUR WAY INTO JESUS

Now, I would like to tell you a story. It introduces a totally different way of leading others to Jesus Christ.

What was the day? Where was I? I have no clear recollection. All I know is I have a strong sense there were people in a large conference, some of whom were not believers. As I was standing before that large audience, out of nowhere I remembered a song from my youth. It was one of the first songs I ever sang after Jesus Christ entered my heart. The words were:

Chapter 6- Singing Your Way Into Jesus

Into my heart,

Into my heart,

Come into my heart, Lord Jesus.

Come in today.

Come in to stay.

Come into my heart, Lord Jesus.

I stumbled through the song before that audience. I sang those very words. Be assured I do not have a good voice. Then I asked the audience to quote the words of that song and then to sing the song with me. I went through the song several times and then I asked everyone to stand and sing that song. Something beautiful and unique was taking place. Here I was, standing before a mixed congregation of those who were saved and those who probably never even heard a clear presentation of Jesus Christ.

I spoke to them all: "If you have never received Jesus Christ as your Savior, speak these words and sing this song. Those of you who are Christians, but you have had some doubts because you never had the opportunity to actually ask Jesus Christ to come into your life, I want you to say these words and sing this song. I also want to say to all the rest of the Christians, say these words and sing this song. It will help us all."

So, I led them in saying the words one sentence at a time. Then I began singing. There was a small group of people who sang the words with me. By the time I had gotten to the end, it seemed everyone was singing those words. We sang once, we sang it another time. I said, "If it is the first time you have ever done this, I want you to come forward." I waited a moment. People began stepping into the aisle. I was astonished at the number of people who came forward. The second thing that held me in awe was the number of people who were crying as they came.

I said, "If you never did this very thing which you are now doing, even though you know you are a Christian but you have had some doubts, you come here and let's sing this song together one more time."................. I watched some very devout Christians start down the aisle.

I have used this song since that day. When an individual seems to be open to everything I have said to them, I give them the words to that song without the music and then ask them to repeat the words. Then, I sing the words without asking the person to join in with me. The chances are excellent that the person has never heard of this song. After that, I ask them to sing the song with me twice all the way through.

No, there is no "bow your head," there is no prayer. Instead, there is singing. I watched people sing their way into the kingdom of God.

No, I still cannot sing well, and I often get mixed up with the words. On the other hand, I have seen people break down weeping, more than any prayer I could have asked them to repeat could ever do.

You can do this when there is no one present but you and the person you are talking to about the Lord. You can even use these words without singing.

It would look like this:

"I would like for you to listen to these words. They are the words to a song." Then, slowly and clearly, you say:

Into my heart,

Into my heart,

Come into my heart, Lord Jesus.

Come in today,

Come in to stay,

Come into my heart, Lord Jesus.

Then say, "Please repeat these words after me."

These words are one of the most effective ways I know of to bring a person into the

Chapter 6- Singing Your Way Into Jesus

experience of receiving Christ. Nor do I know any song that, singing it, will be so effective for salvation or for a brand-new Christian.

As I close this chapter, I will repeat what I have said: Practice! Find a fellow Christian with whom you can practice. Memorize the words to the song and learn the melody.

I walk down the street singing unto my Lord, "Come into my heart, come into my heart, Lord Jesus. Come in today, come in to stay." I do not need to sing that song, but I sing it anyway. I add to that, "I love you Lord; Lord I love you" as quietly, as gently, as lovingly as I possibly can. I strongly recommend that you sing it.

You are the shyest Christian on earth. The very thought of talking to someone else about Jesus Christ terrifies you. Have you ever thought about starting out by saying, "I want to sing you a song. I would like for you to listen to the words. They are very meaningful to me. The words without the melody are 'Come into my heart, come into my heart, come into my heart Lord Jesus.' I said those words once. They changed my life. Divine life entered my life. Divine life, the very life of God, entered my life. I have a life in me that is higher than the world's life or human life. I can also sing these words. I am speaking, of course, about having invited Jesus Christ to come live inside of me."

I would then repeat these words and sing them.

Into my heart,

Into my heart,

Come into my heart, Lord Jesus.

Come in today,

Come in to stay,

Come into my heart, Lord Jesus.

Then continue, "Now it is up to you. Would you like to invite Him to come into your life?"

Depending on the circumstances, I will say, "The words have music to them. I am going to sing them to you."

So, you sing, "Come into my heart,

Come into my heart, Lord Jesus.

Come in today,

Come in to stay,

Come into my heart, Lord Jesus."

Or depending on the circumstances, you leave off the singing part.

There is something else you can do, and that is to make some copies of this song. Keep them in your wallet or your purse, and just casually say to the person, "These are the words that once changed my life and changed it radically. It was the day that I invited Jesus Christ into my life. Give it some thought. Would you

Chapter 6- Singing Your Way Into Jesus

like Jesus Christ to come into your life and bring His divine life into you? Here are the words. If you would like to repeat them, let me know." Then hand them the words.

CHAPTER 7

THE UNBELIEVABLE

There is so much adventure, sometimes downright amazing experiences in leading others to Christ. Of all the unbelievable stories I might tell you, I must mark this as the most unbelievable.

I want very much to tell you this little story. I think the chances of this happening are in the millions, perhaps the billions.

You may recall my telling about a young man who was sitting on the fender of my car parked out in front of the Tabernacle Baptist

Chapter 7- The Unbelievable

Church in the tiny little town called Pickton, Texas.

Now I would like for you to imagine what it is like to fly over greater Los Angeles. I have no idea what the population of Los Angeles was at that time, or even now, but I would venture it would be close to four million by now. Los Angeles is often called the city that is a hundred miles long.

The details are not clear after all this time. All I can tell you is that I had been invited to speak at a conference in greater Los Angeles. As was my way, I did door-to-door evangelism, mostly with ministers. This was to get them acquainted with a visitation program for their church. Also, if invited to a living room, I would sit down and talk to someone present in that home about the Lord.

I rang a doorbell, and the door opened. Please remember that this was in greater Los Angeles, one of the most populous cities in

Chapter 7- The Unbelievable

the country. The man who opened the door recognized me immediately. I also recognized him immediately. It was the young man to whom I had tried to witness there in the front yard of the Tabernacle Baptist Church in Pickton, Texas! I had so utterly failed, if you recall, that it was at that time I decided that, come what may, I was going to find the names of well-known soulwinners and learn from them.

Both of us were stunned, as we remembered what had happened at least five years earlier. He invited me in. As best I can recall the details, I met his wife. We sat down and chatted for a few minutes. I had the marvelous privilege of seeing that young man accept Jesus Christ as his Lord and Savior. Over a thousand miles from Pickton, Texas!

Why am I telling you this story? It was at that time one of the crowning experiences of my entire life.

Chapter 7- The Unbelievable

If all of us shy people can really come to grips with our shyness and begin taking steps which are found in this little book, you will find that surely at least fifty percent of the people you talk to will not be rude to you but give you time to talk to them about the Lord Jesus.

Please go back and check the different things I have asked you to do, as one shy Christian to another.

www.ingramcontent.com/pod-product-compliance
Lightning Source LLC
Chambersburg PA
CBHW030239090526
44586CB00034B/425